The Way of the Fussbudget Is Not Easy

© 1975 United Feature Syndicate, Inc.

Peanuts Parade Paperbacks

1. Who's the Funny-Looking Kid with the Big Nose?
2. It's a Long Way to Tipperary
3. There's a Vulture Outside
4. What's Wrong with Being Crabby?
5. What Makes You Think You're Happy?
6. Fly, You Stupid Kite, Fly!
7. The Mad Punter Strikes Again
8. A Kiss on the Nose Turns Anger Aside
9. Thank Goodness for People
10. What Makes Musicians So Sarcastic?
11. Speak Softly, and Carry a Beagle
12. Don't Hassle Me with Your Sighs, Chuck
13. There Goes the Shutout
14. Always Stick Up for the Underbird
15. It's Hard Work Being Bitter
16. How Long, Great Pumpkin, How Long?
17. A Smile Makes a Lousy Umbrella
18. My Anxieties Have Anxieties
19. It's Great to Be a Super Star
20. Stop Snowing on My Secretary
21. Summers Fly, Winters Walk
22. The Beagle Has Landed
23. And a Woodstock in a Birch Tree
24. Here Comes the April Fool!
25. Dr. Beagle and Mr. Hyde
26. You're Weird, Sir!
27. Kiss Her, You Blockhead!
28. I'm Not Your Sweet Babboo!
29. The Way of the Fussbudget Is Not Easy

The Way of the Fussbudget Is Not Easy

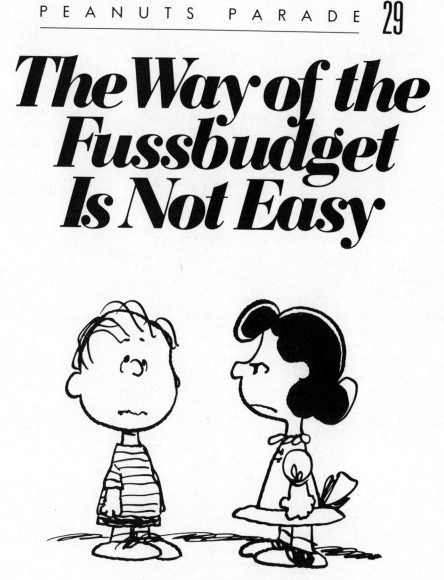

© 1952 United Feature Syndicate, Inc.

by Charles M. Schulz

An Owl Book

Henry Holt and Company / New York

PEANUTS comic strips by Charles M. Schulz
Copyright © 1983, 1984 by United Feature Syndicate, Inc.

All rights reserved, including the right to reproduce this
book or portions thereof in any form.

Published by Henry Holt and Company, Inc.,
521 Fifth Avenue, New York, New York 10175.

Published simultaneously in Canada.

First published in book form in 1986.

Library of Congress Catalog Card Number: 85–82547

ISBN: 0-03-005619-5 (pbk.)

First Edition

Printed in the United States of America

10 9 8 7 6 5 4 3 2 1

© 1966 United Feature Syndicate, Inc.

ISBN 0-03-005619-5

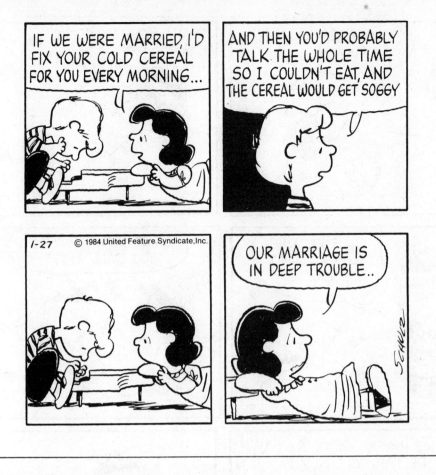

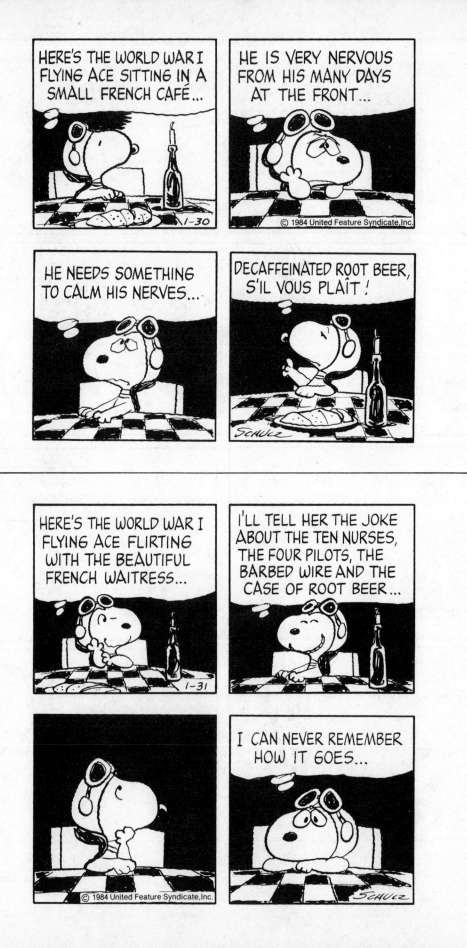

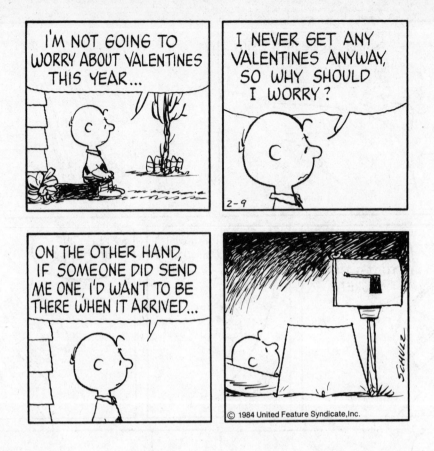

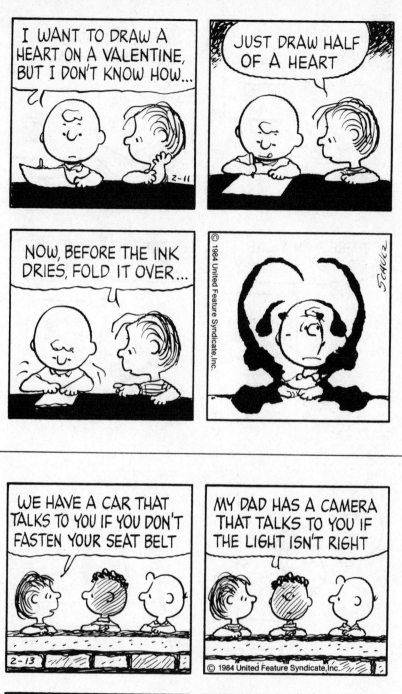

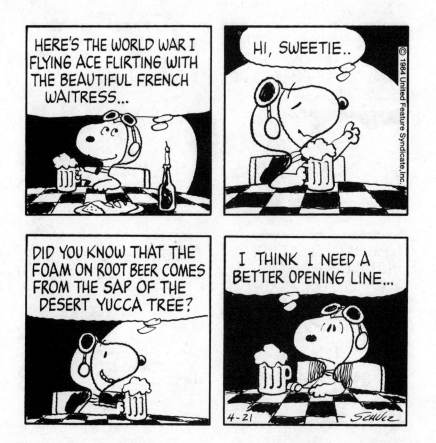

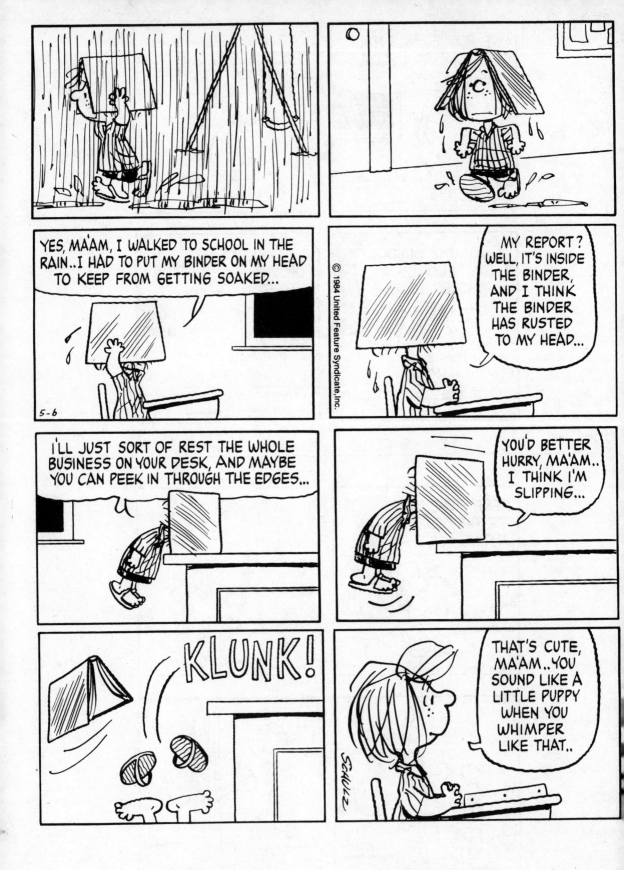

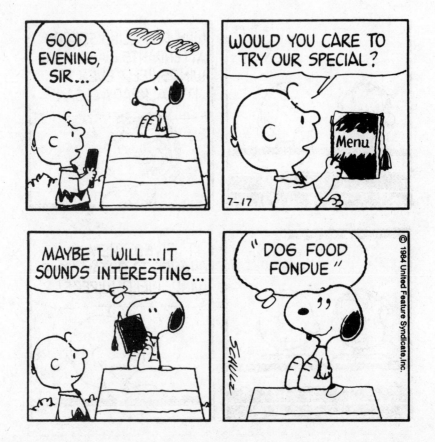

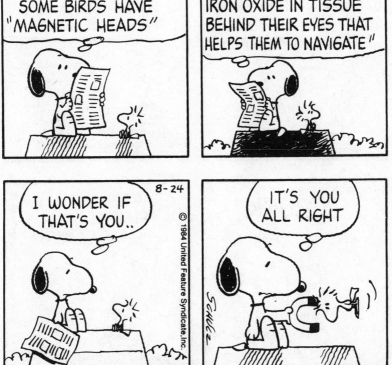

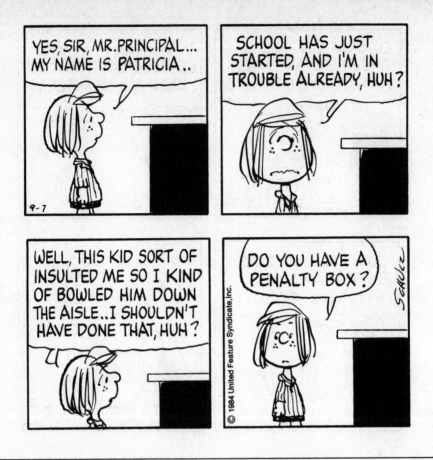

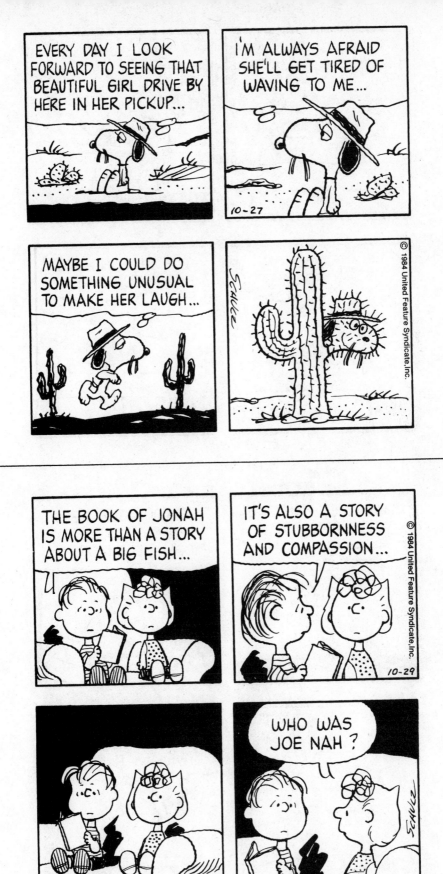

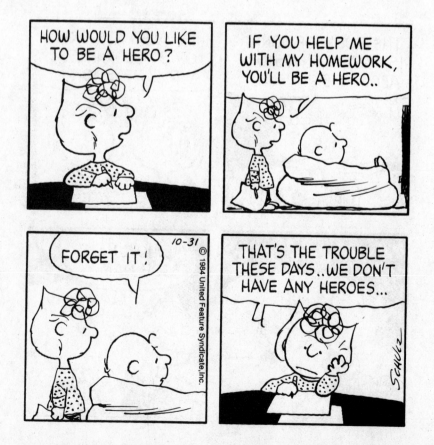

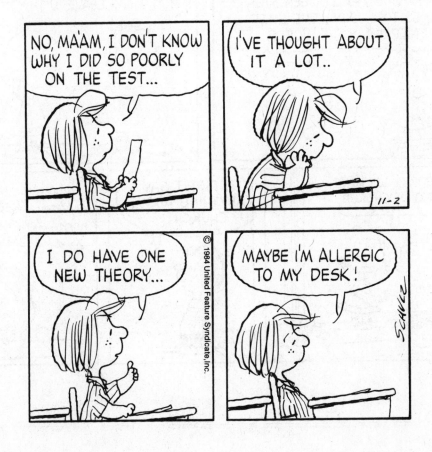

HI, SWEETIE! HI! HI!
Dear Snoopy, After I wave to the girl in the red pickup every day, I usually don't have anything else to do.
So lately I have been knitting some stocking caps for me and my friends.
11-29
© 1984 United Feature Syndicate, Inc.
SCHULZ

He was a huge man with a fierce and wild expression, and eyes
like
a teeny tiny little yellow bird.
© 1984 United Feature Syndicate, Inc.
11-30
SCHULZ

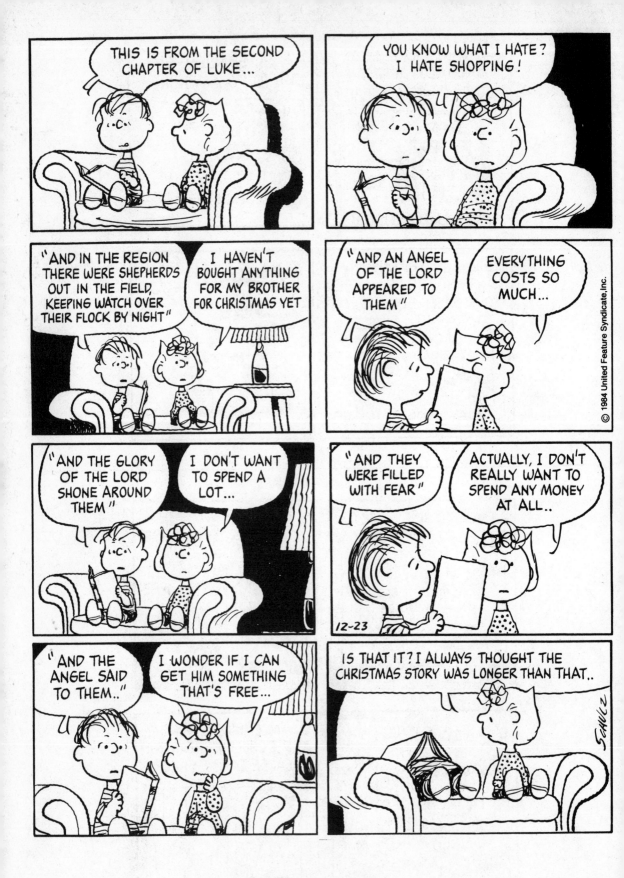